Win
and
Frui

£1-20

The Foremost Home Winemaking Series

General Editor **B. C. A. Turner**

T. Edwin Belt

Wines from Jams and Preserved Fruits

Mills & Boon LIMITED, LONDON
In association with
Home Beer and Wine Making

First published in Great Britain 1971 by
Mills & Boon Limited, 17–19 Foley Street, London
W1A 1DR

ISBN 0 263 51655 5

Made and printed in Great Britain by
C. Nicholls & Company Ltd
The Philips Park Press, Manchester M11 4AU

Contents

Introduction

A Wine for Every Taste

Jams, canned and dried fruits provide the opportunity for winemaking all the year round, and are available in very adequate variety, more than enough to satisfy all requirements. Canned fruit offers the widest choice of ingredients and there are some exotic names to savour, such as guavas, litchis, mango and papaya, if you are inclined toward experiment.

Guavas are a pale yellow fruit, having a foreshortened pear shape. Besides being canned, they are also made into jam. They are juicy and full of small seeds, sharp tasting, and have a very high vitamin C content. Litchis, or lychees, are the size and shape of the plum, a pinkish crimson in colour, and their outside is reminiscent of the pineapple; the pulp is a translucent white, jelly-like, and the canned ones have an acid-sweet flavour. The dried fruit has a nutty, raisin-like flavour. The mango flesh is orange coloured, up to a fifth of its weight is sugar, and it contains vitamins A, B, and C. It is found as a preserve, also canned, and as chutney. Papaya, or paw-paw, has a pink to orange coloured flesh, with a 10% sugar content; it contains an enzyme, papain, which has the power to break down protein, and is used in brewing. The

smaller fruit of the mountain paw-paw is
usually made into jam.

The grape is, of course, well known for its use
in winemaking and various types are available
to us in the dried forms as currants, sultanas
and raisins. These dried forms can be used
alone for winemaking, or in combination with
other fruits, not only for their flavour, but to
provide the foundation for a good
fermentation. As we now have considerable
knowledge of the requirements which will keep
yeast happy in its work of fermentation and the
production of alcohol, we have the
opportunity to produce distinctive British
wines from home-grown and greenhouse
fruits. It should be more generally known that
wine is not only defined as the fermented
juice of grapes – I have a forty year old
dictionary which also defines wine as the liquor
made from the juice of certain fruits and
palms. So don't let anyone tell you that you're
not making a true wine when you're not
trampling on any grapes. The quality of the
end product is in your hands.

The multiplicity of flavour, aroma and colour
offered by fruit, whether as jam, canned, or
dried, does not need any elaboration here, and
applies equally to the wines to be made from
it. The good food value of fruit is not lost in
the process of winemaking.

The amount of sugar, either fermentable or
unfermentable, which you decide to use in

each recipe or formulation will determine
whether you finish up with a dry, medium or
sweet wine. Most of the produce now under
discussion contains natural sugar, and this
will be taken into account when we decide
upon the amount of white household sugar to
be used in our recipes.

Fruits contain acid in varying proportions. The
amount of acid in your finished wine
determines its degree of tartness. It varies not
only from fruit to fruit, and from the degree of
ripeness, but from season to season, and
between different varieties of the same fruit.
Acid is often added to fruit in the preparation
of jam. However, we shall be using sufficient
water in our winemaking to produce a very
considerable dilution in the acid content of
our fruit juices, and since acid is essential to
the well-being of the yeast in its fermentation
duties, most of the formulations will contain
additional acid.

Natural tannin occurs, chiefly in the skin, of
many fruits, and is required in our wine to give
it 'bite'. Here again, our degree of dilution
makes it desirable to add tannin in almost all
cases.

The body of a wine, in terms of its degree of
lightness or of heaviness, will be determined
by the weight of fruit used. When making a
'heavy' as opposed to a 'light' wine, most
people appreciate rather more acid and
tannin in the formulation, since the

corresponding attributes of 'tartness' and 'bite' are masked to a certain extent by the extra body of the wine.

You can choose the alcoholic strength of your wines by the amount of fermentable sugar included in your recipe, but only up to a maximum of about 17% alcohol by volume (30° proof). Stronger wine can be concocted by fortification, namely the straight addition of alcohol to a finished wine. Port wine is a commercial example of this.

A Wine for Each Occasion

The variety of wines which can be produced with fruit as a base is wide, and can complement almost every food. Most palates can also be satisfied when these wines are savoured alone, either as aperitifs or after a meal.

There are no fixed rules as to which wine should accompany any particular dish of food, but it should be of value to learn of those which have earned general acclaim in this respect, and these will be given later. For the moment, it is encouraging to become aware that a cellar of homemade wines can provide a library of bottles from which you, as a discriminating host, will be able to enhance each and every occasion, whether from the social or the gourmet aspect.

The bottles of wine should be kept somewhere

that is adequately ventilated, dry and dark and not subject to extremes of temperature. A cupboard under the staircase, or a boxroom which satisfies these conditions, is all that is necessary. A constant temperature of 7–10°C (45–50°F) is ideal.

An aperitif wine is normally of 14% alcoholic strength by volume, on the sweet side of dry, with a good but not too pronounced bouquet and flavour, clean on the palate, slightly astringent, and of medium body. Aperitifs are designed to stimulate the appetite before a meal.

Table wines are usually the least alcoholic of wines, 10% alcohol by volume being normal. They are fairly thin in texture, light-bodied, delicate, and with a more noticeable acidity. They can range from dry to semi-dry and have a subtle flavour. The red wines are sometimes rich, with a touch of astringency, and the white are occasionally sweet and full-bodied; in both such cases the alcoholic strength is about the same as for an aperitif. The white wines are best served at a temperature of 10°C (50°F) and the red at 18°C (64°F).

Sparkling table wines are often a little stronger, at about 12% alcohol by volume. A minor fermentation is induced in the bottle, so that a champagne bottle should be used and it is essential to wire down the cork or stopper. They are best served cool at about 13°C (55°F).

Social wines are appreciated at a strength
around 14% alcohol by volume, semi-dry,
medium-flavoured and medium-bodied. This
is where we score over the commercial
products, where there is no comparable type
of wine.

Dessert wines are those which have been
fermented out to the maximum naturally
obtainable strength of 17% alcohol by
volume. They are at their best when full-
bodied, rich and sweetish, full-flavoured,
and with a good bouquet. They are usually
served after a meal, or with the cheese and
biscuits.

Shorts or liqueurs are fortified wines, often
made from wines that are strong in alcoholic
content, acidity, tannin and body, but
mild-flavoured. Because of this last quality a
distinctive flavour can be added in the form of
an essence. Sugar syrup and Polish spirit are
the other ingredients used. Such wines have
an alcholic content in excess of 17% by
volume. A less expensive method of making a
liqueur is to freeze out some of the water (if
you have a deep-freezer) from one of your
own dry to dryish wines. Liqueurs are rich,
full-bodied and, of course, strong.

Aperitif Wines can be made from jams, canned
and dried fruit. You can buy special flavours
for addition to these wines if you so wish.
Vermouth is an example in the commercial field.
Table wines, sparkling table wines, social and

dessert wines, can all be made equally well from these same main ingredients. Bananas and forced rhubarb make particularly good bases for wines intended to be fortified into liqueurs.

We will be matching the yeast to the type of wine which we wish to produce with each recipe, bearing in mind the suitability of the main ingredient. You can make your choice, for a start, from the following:

Aperitif wines are: dry Champagne, which is served at cellar temperature; dry and medium-dry Madeira; white Port, which is best served chilled; and dry Sherry, which is also served chilled.

Table wines are:

1   Dry Sherry, which is pale in colour and is best with hors d'oeuvre and soup, or a medium-dry type which is full-bodied and goes well with shellfish.

2   Dry and medium-dry Madeira, to take with soup.

3   White Burgundy to enjoy with fish.

4   Chablis, which is a white, dry, rich and fruity Burgundy, again going well with fish.

5   White Beaujolais, which is also a Burgundy type for complementing a dish of fish.

6   Graves, a dry and white Bordeaux wine, excellent with shellfish.

7   For soup, meat and game, a red, dry and light in acid, Claret is served at room temperature. (This is the name, peculiar to this country, given to a Bordeaux wine).

8   A red, dry and more robust wine than Claret is Burgundy, which is also served at room temperature with soup, meat and game.

9   Hock is a fuller white wine than Moselle, and of similar character.

Sparkling table wines can be red, pink or white, and with an equally wide range of flavours. They are served chilled, to slow down the effervescence.

Social wines are:

1   A very sweet, dark coloured and rich Sherry.

2   A red, dry and fairly robust Burgundy.

3   A dry and white Bordeaux.

4   A sweet and full-bodied white Sauterne.

Dessert wines are:

1   Sweet Champagne, which is served at room temperature.

2   Sweet and rich Sherry.

3   Sweet, rich, full-bodied, golden coloured
Madeira.

4   Medium-dry, red Port.

5   Sweet and full-bodied white Sauterne,
which is the second of the best known
Bordeaux wines.

6   Sweet Tokay.

Stocking Your Own Wine Cellar – the Cost.
Your wines should preferably be stored in bulk
containers, where they mature better than in
individual bottles, as well as taking up less
space. Plastic barrels, complete with tap, are
available in 9.125 and 22.5 litres (2 and 5 gallon
sizes); the smaller at a cost of about £1 and
the larger at just over double that amount.

If, however, you produce your wines in variety,
and 1 gallon (5 litres) at a time, you will need
half a dozen bottles for each lot. You can buy
the bottles if you prefer, but it is sometimes
possible to get them from a licensed restaurant
or your local pub.

Traditionalists may wish to use new corks
for their old bottles, but new plastic stoppers,
which can be used time and again, can also be
bought from your home winemaking supplier.
Corked bottles must be stored on their sides,
in order to keep the corks moist, airtight and

well fitting. A wine rack is almost a necessity
in such circumstances. If you use plastic
stoppers, make sure that they are a good fit;
their advantage is that the bottles can be
stored upright on suitable shelving, and thus
probably take up less room. Plastic bottle
closures give a professional finish to your
corked and stoppered bottles, and bottle labels
are also available to this end. If you use corks,
it is desirable to invest in a corking machine,
and these range in price from 50p and upwards
according to their sophistication. You will
agree that none of the products mentioned is
expensive, and most of them will last for years
even in constant use.

The cost of half a dozen bottles of the wines
described, ranges from £1.15 to £1.40.

The average regular wine drinking family may
be very willing to consume twenty-four dozen
bottles of wine per year, at the right price,
and given the opportunity, and this works out
at the equivalent cost of 50p to 70p per week.
This is on the assumption that you buy
everything from the shops, and does not take
into account the saving on home-made jam
or bottled fruit. This may sound like a lot of
wine to the uninitiated, but pause for a moment
to consider continental wine drinking habits,
and the subject will drop into the right
perspective.

1 How To Make Quality Wines

The Essential Ingredients

The first requirement of a wine is for it to have an alcoholic content. Yeast and sugar are the ingredients used in recipes or formulations as they are properly called, for the production of alcohol. The second requirement is that the yeast must be provided with sustenance to enable it to function to its full capacity. Nutrient salts are added, when necessary, for this purpose. There must be a degree of acidity, and this is provided, when absent, by citric, malic and tartaric acids. Tannin is required to give a wine a slight astringency and 'bite'. Flavour and aroma are imparted by a bulk ingredient, after which the wine is usually named. The amount of alcohol, unfermented sugar, acid, tannin, and flavour, together with the density of the wine, all combine to give it body, without which it would be thin and watery.

A quality wine is the outcome of all these ingredients being present in the correct quantities and proportions.

Later we will discuss how this is to be achieved in the case of each of our three classes of wine; those from jams, canned and dried fruits. Before doing this, however, let us consider the yeasts, sugars, and other essential ingredients available for the purpose of winemaking.

Yeast can be purchased in the form of baker's, brewer's, granulated, tablet, powder, paste and liquid, together with varieties grown on agar jelly, and some from Germany on dried rosehip. Yeasts specifically produced for use in winemaking are generally available in tablet and liquid form, and we shall be using the former in the following recipes. Baker's yeast produces a rapid fermentation, not always desirable in winemaking, and it is not to be recommended for wines intended to have a high alcoholic content. It can also cause off-flavours if left in contact with the young wine for too long. These same remarks can be applied to brewer's yeast which, in addition, can give a bitter residual hop flavour to your wine. The others can be experimented with at your leisure, and on inclination, but as mentioned before we will confine ourselves to the tablet form of specific wine yeasts in these pages. Some liquid and tablet wine yeasts have the advantage that they can be added direct to the must (this is the liquor awaiting the addition of the yeast, all prepared ready for fermentation into wine). Other liquid and tablet wine yeasts have to be prepared at least forty-eight hours before they are required for use, with the aid of a 'starter' solution, for which the required ingredients can be:

$\frac{1}{2}$ oz (14g) Minced sultanas
$\frac{1}{4}$ oz (7g) Sugar
$\frac{1}{2}$ pint (0.25 litres) Water

These particular ingredients have been chosen
because they are the stock-in-trade of the
home winemaker; simmer them together for
fifteen minutes, allow to cool, transfer to a
sterilized bottle, add the yeast at 24°C (75°F)
and then plug the neck with cotton wool.

You could, if you so wished, use fruit juice
and sugar; malt extract, acid and sugar, or
any such complete yeast food which will
reactivate the yeast.

Tablet wine yeast is being made available in
ever increasing selection, but a good foundation
of types prior to experimentation on your own
is as follows:

Aperitif Sherry, Madeira, Champagne, Port.

Table Sherry, Madeira, Burgundy, Chablis,
Beaujolais, Graves, Bordeaux, Hock.

Sparkling Table Champagne.

Social Sherry, Burgundy, Bordeaux, Sauterne.

Dessert Champagne, Sherry, Madeira, Port,
Bordeaux, Tokay, Sauterne.

Tokay is a good type of yeast to use use with
all red wines, since these are more successful

with a fast fermentation and Tokay yeast is an uniquely high temperature toleration yeast. It gives an unusually firm, flaked deposit and, in common with all yeasts should not be subjected to a high initial concentration of alcohol, as will be described in the method of making dessert wines.

None of the above named yeasts will produce a wine similar to their stated name from other ingredients, unless their complementary grapes are used, but they will bring out the natural flavour of a similar formulation, and will give you the best opportunity of producing a wine of 17% alcoholic content by volume, which is the most you can hope for from the fermentation process. They also throw a firm sediment, and do not readily impart off-flavours. Stronger wines in the 'shorts' class are produced by the addition of Polish spirit, and you must be sure to increase the other ingredients of the wine when formulating it, in order to maintain a correct balance with the alcohol, as was mentioned when we described 'body' as applied to wine.

The amount of yeast to use in any given volume of must is not critical. A good, adequate and steady fermentation cannot be expected if too small an amount of yeast is used, since it will take time to multiply itself into a sufficient 'labour force'. On the other hand, too great a surplus of yeast will increase the chance of off-flavours developing. The tablet form is usually used at the rate of one

per gallon (5 litres); baker's and brewer's
yeast at 1 oz (30 grammes) per gallon (5 litres);
the granulated type at one teaspoonful per
gallon (5 litres). When yeast is to be prepared
in a 'starter' solution, and the quantity of
yeast supplied is said to be sufficient for 5
gallons (22.5 litres), it is advisable to use it all
in the starter, and then divide the starter, after
a good stirring, into smaller fractions of not
less than one third per gallon (5 litres).

Ordinary household granulated white sugar
(sucrose) is eminently suitable for winemaking.
Invert sugar can be used if you wish, but it
costs more and its only advantage is in
causing an earlier start to the fermentation
process.

Nutrient salts can be bought in tablet and
powder form, and should then be used as
directed by the manufacturer. We will now
describe the functions of these salts, since
they will help us to understand the build up of
our formulations. Amino acids are a
constituent of jams, canned and dried fruits,
and are a nutrient requirement for yeast, but
yeast also requires nitrogen with which to
sustain life. (Yeast is, of course, one of the
lowest form of life.) This we can conveniently
supply by adding ammonium phosphate at the
rate of one teaspoonful per gallon (5 litres).
The fruit juices which we shall be using should
contain the vitamin requirements of the
yeast, but to be sure in this respect, and thus
avoid a 'stuck' fermentation (so called when

fermentation ceases before all the sugar has been converted into alcohol) you may like to add a 3 mg size vitamin B_1 tablet per gallon (5 litres) of your must. These Benerva tablets are also available in 10, 25, and 50 mg strengths.

Citric, malic and tartaric acids, when not present as a complete trio in the fruit being used, should be augmented by any one, two, or all three as the case may be. The melon is the only common fruit which does not contain acid. The grape is unique in that it alone contains tartaric acid. Jam, and in particular, home-made jams, have citric acid added during the manufacturing process. This acid normally takes the form of lemon juice, and eight lemons are equivalent to 1 oz (30 grammes) of the crystals purchased at your chemist. The acids in combination are required to ensure good growing conditions for the yeast, and to improve the keeping quality of the finished wine. They are required in the must, either as a natural fruit constituent or as an additive, in the proportions of 1:2:2 citric, malic, tartaric. Sweet wines require a little more acid, say half as much again as dry wines.

These are the main acid constituents of some fruits:

Apple – malic   Cherry – malic
Apricot – citric and malic   Cranberry – citric
Banana – citric and malic   Currants – citric
Blackberry – malic   Damson – malic

Fig – citric   Pineapple – citric
Gooseberry – malic   Plum – malic
Grape – malic and tartaric   Prune – malic
Grapefruit – citric   Quince – citric
Lemon – citric   Raspberry – citric
Orange – citric   Rhubarb – malic
Peach – malic   Strawberry – citric
Pear – citric   Tomato – citric

Fruits high in acidity are red and white currants, rhubarb, Morello cherry, gooseberry and raspberry.

Figs and dates are low in acid content.

Average amounts of acid are to be found in grapes, apples, plums, blackberries and strawberries. Such fruits can have acid added in accordance with the basic formulations, as will those low in acid content, since we effect a very considerable dilution of the juices to bring them up to a volume of 1 gallon (5 litres).

Tannin assists in the clearing and maturing of your wine, and the 'bite' of a quality wine comes from this source. Most fruits contain very little or no tannin, although pear peelings are rich in it. It is available as grape tannin powder from the suppliers of home winemaking ingredients, and can also be obtained if a few oak leaves are added to the must. Grape tannin is the additive of choice in fruit wines, but tannin is readily provided in an emergency by adding half a teaspoonful of tea to the 1 gallon (5 litres) of must. In such a case, scald a teabag with a pint (0.5 litres) of water, leave to brew and cool, and then use half of this amount to each gallon (5 litres) of must. This way there is no trouble with the tea leaves, which can be removed intact in their bag from the jug or other container in which the tea has been brewed.

Jams and canned fruits are comparatively expensive, and extra body in, and improvement in the quality of, the wine can be achieved by substituting concentrated grape juice. Dried fruits, other than the grape derivatives, are also relatively expensive, and currants, raisins and sultanas are a useful additive to such formulations. Both grape juice and the dried grapes contain natural sugar, and the sugar given in the basic formulation must be reduced accordingly. Grape concentrate contains $\frac{1}{2}$ lb (250 grammes) of sugar per pint (0.625 litre).

We will now decide upon the general requirements for the formulation of jam, canned and dried fruit wines, in the light of all these facts, and the natural constituents of the ingredients.

Using Jam
All jam and similar preserves contain pectin, otherwise the pulped fruit would not have set – pectin is the gelatinizing agent. When pectin has had to be added during the manufacture of the jam, due to a pectin deficiency of the fruit used, there may be loss of flavour, which is

sometimes made good in the commercial field
by the use of artificial flavourings. The
fruits listed below have a high natural pectin
content, and consequently, the jam
manufacturer is unlikely to have spoilt their
natural flavour:
apples (cooking), blackcurrants, crab apples,
damsons, gooseberries, lemons, loganberries,
oranges (bitter), plums, quinces, redcurrants.

The fruits which are likely to have suffered a
very considerable addition of pectin during
manufacture into jam are:
blackberries, cherries, raspberries, rhubarb,
strawberries, and particularly those jams
containing whole fruits.

Most of our native fruits not so far mentioned
fall between these two categories. It follows
that, if you are new to jam winemaking, the
first list of fruits is the one from which to
choose your jam. Pectolase, Pectinol, are some
of the trade names for pectin destroying
enzymes which must be used in all jam wines
if haze in the finished wine is to be avoided.

Home-made jam contains 9 oz (560 grammes)
of sugar to the pound (kilogramme) and no
additional sugar is required in the basic
formulations which we shall be using.
Commercial jams do not rely on their sugar
content to prevent contamination by moulds,
but on sterilization of the surface of the jam
and the use of hermetically sealed jars instead.
This enables the jams to be less sweet than

the home-made product. Up to 40% of the
sugar used is converted into invert sugar by
the jam making process. This assures the
winemaker of an early start to his jam wine
fermentation. You may anticipate that
commercial jams will contain between 6 and
8 oz (450 to 500 grammes) of sugar to the
pound (kilogramme). However, the use of a
hydrometer will determine the amount to be
added for each particular wine, as is shown in
the Alcoholic Strength Chart on page 36.

Amino acids are a natural constituent of jam,
and indeed of all fruits, and should ensure a
good fermentation.

Ammonium phosphate is required for jam
wines, the quantity being one level
teaspoonful per gallon (5 litres).

It is a statutory regulation that no commercial
jam or marmalade shall contain any added
acid other than citric, malic, or tartaric; one is
tempted to believe that this regulation was
made with jam winemaking in mind. A pH
value of 3.5 is, moreover, the optimum for the
correct setting of jam, and corresponds
within narrow limits to the pH requirement for
wine. We have to dilute the jam for our
purpose, of course, and all we have to ensure
is that we do not upset this almost ideal
degree of acidity. A short explanation of the
meaning of pH values will be given later. The
quantities of added acid given in the basic
formulations should be regarded as maximum

amounts. A level teaspoonful of these acids weighs about $\frac{1}{6}$ oz (5 grammes).

Tannin is present mainly in the skins of fruit, and the skin is sometimes removed prior to jam making. In these cases, grape tannin must be added to the must for the wine is to have astringency and 'bite'. Our degree of dilution of the jam in winemaking, ensures that all you need to do when tannin is known to be present in a jam is to go easy on the amount of added tannin given in the formulations. Jams rich in tannin are: elderberry, bilberry, damson, plum, sloe. Tannin is required in jam wines in the proportion of half to one teaspoonful of grape tannin per gallon (5 litres) of must.

The fruit in the jam will provide reasonable body, without further addition in this respect, unless you prefer full-bodied wines.

Using Canned Fruit
Some fruits are deficient in natural pectin, and if you are just starting to make wine from canned fruit it is a good idea to use these fruits, and thus ensure without further ado, a haze free wine. Such fruits are: bilberry, blackberry, cherry, elderberry, medlar, pear, raspberry, rhubarb, strawberry.

All other fruits require the addition of a pectin destroying enzyme.

Home-made 'canned' fruit is usually bottled, in chunks, or as pulp, purée, or syrup. The natural sugar in the fruit chunks is normally augmented with $\frac{1}{4}$ lb (250 grammes) of sugar to the pound (kilogramme) of fruit. The pulp bottling of fruit does not entail any addition to its natural sugar content, and purée likewise has only the natural sugar content. Syrup contains about $4\frac{1}{2}$ lb (2.0 kg) of sugar to the gallon (5 litres) and must be diluted for winemaking.

Commercial canned fruit usually contains a little less sugar than that just described. Examples of the percentage sugar content by weight of such canned fruits are:
apricot 16%, fruit salad 30%, loganberry 26%, pear 16%, pineapple 16%.

Commercial syrup has a sugar content similar to the home-made variety, but it can also be bought unsweetened.

Our winemaking, from canned fruit, will thus call for the addition of all or a part of the total weight of sugar required to produce any given strength of wine.

Amino acids are a natural constituent of fruits, and no further action is needed on our part in this respect.

Ammonium phosphate will be added to the extent of one teaspoonful per gallon (5 litres) of wine must.

Citric, malic and tartaric acids are required in

the proportions of 1:2:2, and one or more will
be added to the must according to their
presence in, or absence from the fruit being
used. The degree of dilution with water is
such that only an exceptionally acid fruit will
make a quality wine, without the addition of
acid on our part.

Tannin will be added to nearly all our musts.
It is sometimes present in adequate amount
in the unprepared fruit, such as in pear skins,
but is removed with the skins before canning
or bottling is done. Fruits which remain whole
throughout this process, and which will yield
an adequate amount of tannin are:
elderberry, bilberry, damson, plum, sloe.
Otherwise we will add half to one teasponnful
of grape tannin per gallon (5 litres) of must.

The fruits which we are using will provide
reasonable body in themselves, but in the case of
the elderberry, for example, an unpleasant
excess of tannin can be avoided by substituting
part of this fruit by, say, blackberries on a
weight for weight basis. By this means, a light,
dry elderberry wine can be made palatable.
Concentrated grape juice, as an additive, will
give heavier bodied wines.

Using Dried Fruit
The commercial dried fruits which are
sufficiently free from pectin as to make a
haze free wine without the use of a pectin
destroying enzyme are cherries, bilberries, and
elderberries. If you dry your own fruit in times

of glut, when it is very cheap or free for the taking, then you can add the following to the three last named fruits: blackberries, pears, raspberries, rhubarb and strawberries, which are not available from retail sources.

The use of a pectin destroying enzyme is necessary for all other commercial dried fruits, and in particular for the pectin rich cooking and crab apples. The following home dried fruits, not available from retail sources, are also very rich in pectin: blackcurrants, damsons, gooseberries, loganberries, plums and quinces.

Sugar most be included in the formulation of all dried fruit wines, to a greater or lesser extent according to the natural sugar content of the fruit in its dried form. The drying of fruit effects a form of preservation similar to that achieved by jam making – partial removal of the water content effects a concentration of the sugar as syrup, and of a strength sufficient to inhibit the growth of bacteria. The percentage weight of sugar in some commonly used dried fruits is as follows: currants 63%, dates 64%, figs 53%, peaches 53%, prunes 40%, raisins 64%, sultanas 65%.

Amino acids are present, in adequate amounts for winemaking, in dried fruits.

One teaspoonful of ammonium phosphate per gallon (5 litres) of must will satisfy the nutrient needs of the yeast.

The main acid constituents of fruits were
given earlier. The amount of natural acid is
high in cherries, low in figs and dates, and
average in apples, the grape derivatives, and
other dried fruits on the market. If you've
dried your own gooseberries, raspberries, or
rhubarb, these also have a high acid content.
Owing to the high degree of dilution of our
musts, all that this means is that the amounts
recommended in the basic formulations should
be added, except in the case of rhubarb, when
the oxalic acid present must be removed. It is
worth knowing that forced rhubarb contains
an appreciably smaller amount of this
unwanted acid.

Tannin should be included in the formulation
of all dried fruit wines, except for elderberry,
bilberry and sloe. If you've dried your own
damsons and plums, these do not require the
addition of tannin either. Grape tannin is used
at the rate of half to one teaspoonful per
gallon (5 litres) of must.

The dried grape derivatives – currants, raisins
and sultanas – can be added to the
formulations of other dried fruit wines, in
order to improve the quality and increase the
body of the finished wine, but don't forget to
allow for the natural sugar content which these
will add to the formulation.

Now that we have made clear the general
principles to be followed in the formulation of
our wines, we will proceed to discuss the

general principles to be followed in the
method of production.

The Method

Principles
To avoid repetition throughout the recipes, we
will set out the principles according to which
we shall be working, and this will provide a
reference for augmenting the bare bones of
the methods set out under the formulations.

Sterilization of all our equipment is the first
essential. This is effected by thorough rinsing
with a solution made up of 1½ oz (50 grammes)
of sodium metabisulphite and 4 oz (125
grammes) of citric acid per gallon (5 litres) of
water. Allow the equipment, which will include
your wine bottles, to drip-dry.

Sterilization of ingredients is equally
important. Whenever boiling water is used,
this condition is fulfilled. However, most fruits
contain pectin, and pectin destroying enzymes
demand a temperature below 66°C (151°F) if
they are to live and play their part in the
production of haze free wines; consequently
three Campden tablets per gallon (5 litres) of
must are used as a sterilizing agent when
boiling water is not used.

The type of wine which we intend to make will
determine the amount of sugar required in the
must. We have already discussed the natural
and added sugar content of jams, canned and

dried fruits, and this must be taken into
account when we are determining the total
sugar content required in the musts of various
wines. This is given in the table below.

		per gallon	per 5 litres
10% alcohol by volume	=	2 lb 0 oz	1.00 kg
12% ,, ,, ,,	=	2 lb 8 oz	1.20 kg
14% ,, ,, ,,	=	2 lb 12 oz	1.40 kg
17% ,, ,, ,,	=	3 lb 4 oz	1.65 kg

We now need to find out how much sugar will
have to be added to the must in order to bring
it up to these concentrations. It is not
possible to be precise regarding the sugar
content of jams marketed by various
manufacturers. The sugar content of fruits
varies from one strain to another, from one
country or even county of origin to the next,
and from season to season, not to mention
the number of hours of sunshine which can
appreciably affect the sugar content of the
same fruit. Grape wines have their vintage
years, of course, and this is equally true of the
wines which we make with other fruits. It
follows that we must test each must for sugar
content if we aim to put our wines in the
quality class.

A hydrometer floated in a hydrometer jar
containing a sample of the juice is used to
determine the amount of sugar in our must.
The specific gravity reading obtained, is related
to the sugar content of the juice, and in

accordance with the accompanying Alcoholic
Strength Chart, gives the amount of sugar to
be added for each type of wine.

Our aim is to ferment to dryness (change all the
sugar into alcohol), and medium to sweet
wines will be obtained by the addition of
lactose, a non-fermentable sugar. A
convenient time to add the lactose is at the
moment of filling the storage containers,
whether jars, barrels, or bottles, or when
filling the decanter, since it is a widespread
practice to decant all wines, white as well as
red. The lactose is added, dissolved in the
minimum volume of water, in the proportion of
$\frac{1}{2}$ to 4 oz per gallon (15 to 125 grammes per 5
litres) of wine, according to the sweetness and
heaviness of the finished wine required.

Wines containing up to 14% alcohol by volume
will normally ferment out to dryness, given a
suitable formulation and a correct method,
but stronger wines will repay special attention.
The weight of sugar required to be fermented
will be 3 lb 4 oz (1.65 kg) in a gallon (5 litres) of
must. The procedure to be adopted must take
into consideration the fact that natural sugar
is present in fruit. The first thing to do,
therefore, is to take a hydrometer reading.
Next, consult the Alcoholic Strength Chart,
and make a note of the weight of household
sugar to be included in your 6 pints (4 litres) of
must for the initial fermentation. Allow this
fermentation to proceed for four days,
stirring three times a day. Then syphon into a

fermentation jar, and fit an airlock. When the fermentation has slowed down (after about a further three days or specific gravity 1.010), add about half of the rest of the sugar, but only after it has been dissolved in 1 pint (0.5 litre) of water, brought briefly to the boil and allowed to cool. After the ferment has slowed down once more, the vessel is topped up to the 1 gallon (5 litres) mark with the remainder of the sugar in solution as previously described. Racking is carried out after seven days, then after fourteen days, and the syphon is made to deliver into a funnel, so that a cascade into the fermentation jar occurs. Thereafter, rack monthly in the same manner until fermentation is complete.

A 'stuck ferment', in which fermentation has ceased although sugar is still present in the must, should not happen with the conscientious winemaker, but we can all make mistakes, and in the face of such an occurence make up a yeast starter solution and, when it is going well, add an equal amount of the 'stuck' wine. When this is fermenting satisfactorily, double up with more wine, and continue this doubling up process as each batch gets into its stride fermentation-wise, until all the 'stuck' wine has been transferred to the new fermentation.

The degree of acidity required in our wines is measured in pH units. The neutral point between acidity/alkalinity is pH7. Hence the lower the pH value under 7, the greater the degree of acidity. In the stronger wines, in particular, we must provide good living conditions for the yeast if it is not to be inhibited and leave us with a weaker (and sweetish rather than dry) wine than it is our intention to produce. The pH value required is 3.3, with an allowance of 0.1 either way. There are acid testing kits on the home winemaking

Alcoholic Strength Chart

Specific Gravity of Must at 21°C (70°F)	Ounces (grammes) of additional sugar to be included in 1 gallon (5 litres) of must to increase potential alcoholic content to 10, 12, or 14% by volume			Sugar to be included in 6 pints (4 litres) of must to increase initial potential alcoholic content to 10% for 17% wines
	10%	12%	14%	
1.015	27 (850)	34 (1070)	40 (1260)	20 (680)
1.020	24 (760)	31 (980)	37 (1165)	18 (608)
1.025	22 (690)	29 (910)	35 (1100)	16 (552)
1.030	19 (600)	26 (820)	32 (1010)	14 (480)
1.035	16 (500)	23 (720)	29 (910)	12 (400)
1.040	14 (440)	21 (660)	27 (850)	10 (352)
1.045	12 (380)	19 (600)	25 (790)	9 (304)
1.050	10 (315)	17 (535)	23 (720)	7 (252)
1.055	8 (250)	15 (470)	21 (660)	6 (200)
1.060	6 (190)	13 (410)	19 (600)	4 (152)
1.065	4 (130)	11 (350)	17 (535)	3 (104)
1.070	2 (60)	9 (280)	15 (425)	1 (48)
1.075		7 (220)	13 (370)	
1.080		5 (160)	11 (310)	
1.085		2 (60)	8 (250)	
1.090			6 (195)	
1.095			4 (130)	
1.100			2 (65)	

market which come with full instructions for their use, so that there is no need to elaborate further on this subject, except to mention that precipitated chalk (1 oz per gallon – 30 grammes per 5 litres) will reduce acid content, and that citric acid is most suitable for increasing the acid content.

Jams contain up to 9 oz (560 grammes) of sugar in the pound (kilogramme); canned fruit and concentrated grape juice up to $4\frac{1}{2}$ lb (2 kilogrammes) in 1 gallon (5 litres); dried fruit up to 10 oz (620 grammes) in the pound (kilogramme). Use your hydrometer to ascertain the specific gravity of the must, and include the weight of sugar shown opposite this figure under the required wine.

It has been mentioned that jams, canned and dried fruits provide their own body in a wine. Some of this body can be added to by the cheaper dried fruits, such as the grape derivatives, or by grape juice concentrate, in the interests of economy, or with a view to improving the quality of the finished wine. Whatever weights of these body additives are used, their natural sugar content must be taken into account, and the weight of household sugar to be used will be reduced accordingly. In the case of jam, additives free of natural sugar content would have to be used unless part of the jam is replaced.

Rohament P for producing full-bodied wines, must be mentioned since it pulps the whole fruits (such as strawberries) contained in jams, and the segments to be found in canned fruits, as well as in dried whole fruits. This it does without the loss of vitamins, colour or flavour, and without boiling. It should be used in conjunction with Pectolase or Pectinol, and with the acid required for the formulation of the wine. The Rohament P and the Pectolase are each used in the proportion of 1 teaspoonful per 5 lb (2.5 grammes per 2.5 kilogrammes) of fruit. The procedure is to stir the powders into the water in which the fruit is immersed, leave at room temperature for twenty-four hours, and then heat up briefly to boiling point and press out the juice while still hot. Starch haze can be prevented from appearing in apple and similar wines by the addition of $\frac{1}{2}$ teaspoonful (2.5 grammes) per 20 lb (10 kgs) of fruit, of Fungal Amylase 2209 – 10%, at the same time as the Rohament P and/or Pectolase.

It will be appreciated that metal or lead glazed vessels subject to attack by acids, must not be used in this or in other winemaking processes involving acids. Aluminium, stainless steel and plastic vessels are readily obtainable and are acid resistant.

The above mentioned process will also give the maximum flavour release from fruit, and when delicate flavours are involved, such as when using gooseberries, it is always preferable to use the cool water method of extraction.

Yeast is killed at temperatures in excess of 38°C (100°F), and it is important, therefore, to allow all musts to cool to 21°C (70°F) before adding the yeast. This is the best temperature at which to keep the yeast happy in its work of primary fermentation, and fluctuations should be avoided. Secondary fermentations are best carried on at 18°C (64°F). At 7°C (45°F) the regular wine yeast ceases to function and can be kept in a dormant state in the refrigerator until required for use. Fermentation in the bottle for the production of sparkling table wine should be at a temperature of 7°C (45°F). Tokay is an exceptional yeast in that it works best at a temperature of 33°C (91°F), and so effectively that its work is normally completed within a fortnight.

It is a comparatively simple matter to set your immersion heater to function at 33°C. Bring a deep container of water to that temperature using your thermometer, remove from the heat, immerse the heater, and adjust the screw on the thermostat until the warning light comes on; you are then ready to ferment your wine with Tokay yeast.

When preparing a yeast starter, all the ingredients except the yeast are brought to the boil in the water, and simmered for five minutes. The yeast is added when the mixture has cooled to 21°C (70°F).

The vinometer must be mentioned here, because it is not always used and consequently will not be referred to elsewhere. If you are sufficiently curious to wish to check the alcoholic content of your wines, you should obtain a vinometer. It is particularly suitable for use by the producer of dry wines (that's us, for we add the sweetening, when required, afterwards). A sugar content will give an inaccurate reading because the vinometer works on the principle of capillary attraction, and we wish to measure the alcohol and not the sugar. The vinometer is retailed with full instructions for its use, and we need not pursue the matter any further here, except to say that it is an interesting little instrument and costs only about 50p.

Do not fail to store your red wines in brown or green coloured bottles. Keep the light away from them by this or other means when storing in bulk, if they are not to lose their colour. The fermentation jar should also be protected from daylight. A sheet of brown paper tied around it is effective if you haven't a dark cupboard.

We will now discuss the principles involved in making liqueurs, since these do not fall within wine-making properly so-called but are more of an adjunct – and a worthwhile one too. Any wine with a high alcoholic content, of good body, and of weak flavour, can be used for this purpose. Banana and sultana, banana and raisin, and forced rhubarb wines are worth making with fortification specifically in view.

Our added ingredients are Polish spirit, sugar
and a flavouring essence. Vodka is the same
as Polish spirit. The spirit is available at 100°
and 140° proof. Choose a liqueur to make
from those which bear some resemblance to
the wine being used, if only in colour. Your
wine should be, for preference, 30° proof (17%
alcohol by volume).

A spirit bottle contains 26.6 fl oz (755 cc).
Put one teaspoonful of the flavouring essence
into the bottle, followed by 6 fl oz (175 cc) of
cool sugar syrup, this last coming from your
stock solution of 2 lb (900 grammes) of sugar
dissolved at boiling point in 1 pint (600 cc) of
water. Now add the amount of spirit which is
required to give your chosen strength of liqueur,
and in accordance with the accompanying
Degrees Proof Chart; then top up with wine.
Cork, shake to mix, and you can get out your
liqueur glasses a week later. This will form a
basis for experimentation to suit your own
taste. If the bottle of flavouring essence
carries instructions for the amount of essence
to use, follow those instructions for the
manufacturer knows the strength of his
products better than his new customers.
You can then use your own discretion in
accordance with the results obtained.

Degrees Proof Chart
To fortify 30° proof wine with 100° or 140° proof
Polish spirit: for the desired alcoholic content
of your liqueur, use spirit to the amounts given
overleaf: per 26.6 fl oz (755 cc) bottle.

Liqueur strength	100° proof spirit	140° proof spirit
40° proof;	3 fl oz (80 cc)	2 fl oz (50 cc)
50° "	6 fl oz (160 cc)	4 fl oz (100 cc)
60° "	9 fl oz (250 cc)	5 fl oz (150 cc)
70° "	11 fl oz (330 cc)	7 fl oz (200 cc)
80° "	15 fl oz (410 cc)	9 fl oz (260 cc)
90° "	18 fl oz (490 cc)	11 fl oz (310 cc)

This is the alcoholic range covered by
commercial liqueurs, but a halt is usually
called at 70° proof by the prudent home
liqueur maker.

Practice

All Wines Except Dessert
1   All the equipment to be used is
sterilized by a thorough rinsing in the
sulphite and acid solution, followed by
drip-drying.

2   All unprepared dried fruit is put into a
colander and rinsed with cold running water.

3   Sterilize and extract the flavour from:
(a) Jam, jelly, purée, conserve and marmalade,
by pouring 4 pints (3 litres) of boiling water
over it while contained in a plastic bucket.
Cover and allow to cool to room temperature.
Add Rohament P (if lump fruit is present),
Pectolase, and the acids, and leave at room
temperature, with frequent stirring, for
twenty-four hours. Then heat up briefly to
boiling point, in a boiler, and strain through a
filter bag, into the bucket. Finally, cover with a
sheet of linen.

(b) Canned fruit, by mashing it up in a plastic
bucket with the juice, adding 4 pints (3 litres)
of previously boiled water, cooled to room
temperature. Add Rohament P, Pectolase,
three Campden tablets and the acids, and
continue as described above.

(c) Fruit juice, sweetened or unsweetened, by bringing it briefly to the boil, pouring into a plastic bucket, and when cooled to room temperature, adding Pectolase and the acids. Dilute with previously boiled water as required, but leave out the same number of pints (litres) as you will be using pounds ($\frac{1}{2}$ kilos) of sugar. It is then left for twenty-four hours at room temperature, with frequent stirring.

(d) Dried fruit, by putting it through a mincing machine, and then proceeding as for jam.

4   Make up to the gallon (5 litres) mark with boiled and cooled water, and take a hydrometer reading at 21°C (70°F). If the main ingredients contain sugar, adjust the sugar content as necessary, using the Alcoholic Strength Chart; dissolve the sugar in the minimum of water, or in a little of the must, brought briefly to the boil and then cooled to 21°C. Stir in the grape tannin, ammonium phosphate and the yeast. If a yeast starter is being used, this will have been prepared forty-eight hours previously. Cover with a linen sheet to let the air in and to keep the vinegar fly out.

5   Leave this primary aerobic (with air) fermentation in progress for three days for 10%, five days for 12%, and seven days for 14% alcohol by volume wines, keeping a steady temperature of 21°C (70°F) for white wines, and 24°C (75°F) for rich red wines – this last with the

use of an immersion heater, thermostatically controlled. Do not exceed these temperatures, and if the must is merely kept at room temperature it will come to no harm. Stir three times each day. This fermentation can be vigorous, and is best conducted in a 2 gallon (10 litre) plastic bucket, which will ensure that there is no overspill.

6   Syphon into a fermentation jar, topping up to the neck with boiled and cooled water, if required, and fit a fermentation lock. Keep at 18°C (64°F), or at room temperature, for this secondary anaerobic (without air) fermentation.

7   Rack (syphon off from the less or solids at the bottom of the jar) after a month. Top up the liquid in the jar as before. It is just possible that fermentation will now have ceased (no more bubbles through the fermentation lock), but it can go on for many more weeks. Keep the end of the syphon tube at the bottom of the container which is being filled, so as to minimize the absorption of oxygen. If making a sparkling table wine, save some of the yeast deposit in a small bottle in the refrigerator.

8   Rack again after a further month if the fermentation is still proceeding. The top of the receiving vessel must, of course, be at a lower level than the bottom of the discharging vessel. The syphon is started by sucking on the discharge end of the tube. More hygienic

methods are perhaps possible, but it might be a pity to miss the occasional, inadvertent, mouthful of young wine. Do not allow the other end of the clear plastic tube to disturb the sediment in the discharging vessel – a glass U-bend is helpful in this respect. Top up with cool, previously boiled, water.

9   Rack again after a month, if bubbling has not ceased before. You can now replace the fermentation lock by a small square of polythene wrapping material secured by a rubber band. In the event of any further sedimentation, rack again; top up as before.

10   Bottle, or syphon into bulk containers after a total winemaking time of six months, and store at a temperature of about 7–10°C (45–50°F). If making a sparkling table wine, make a yeast starter bottle from the refrigerated yeast at least three days before bottling, and add a teaspoonful of this starter (after stirring well), together with a teaspoonful of sugar, to each champagne bottle, and wire down. Champagne bottles must be used – wine bottles will burst under the considerable pressure of the carbon dioxide gas, which provides the effervescence in this wine. Add lactose solution for 'sweeter than dry' wines, as previously described.

Dessert Wines

1   Sterilize all equipment as described above.

2   Put dried fruit in a colander and give a
cold running water rinse.

3   Sterilize and extract the flavour from:

(a) Jam, jelly, purée, conserve, and
marmalade, by pouring 4 pints (3 litres) of
boiling water over it while contained in a
plastic bucket. Cover and leave to cool to room
temperature. Add Rohament P (if lump fruit
is present), Pectolase, and the acids, and keep
at room temperature, with frequent stirring,
for twenty-four hours. Then heat up briefly
to boiling point and strain through a filter bag
into the bucket. Then cover with a sheet of
linen and leave to cool. In the particular case
of jam, with which we are concerned in these
pages, use 3 lb (1.5 kg) of jam at this stage.
At stage 7 repeat this stage 3 process, but
using only 1¼ lb (0.625 kg) of jam prepared
twenty-four hours previously, and add it to the
fermentation in lieu of the usual sugar
solution. At stage 8, repeat stage 7 as just
described, using the remaining 1¼ lb (0.625
kg) of jam.

(b) Canned fruit, by mashing it up with the
juice contained in a plastic bucket, adding
4 pints (3 litres) of previously boiled water
cooled to room temperature, Rohament P,
Pectolase (if pectin is present), and the acids,
and proceeding as described above.

(c) Fruit juice, sweetened or unsweetened, by

bringing it briefly to the boil, pouring into a
plastic bucket, and when cooled to room
temperature, add Pectolase (if pectin is
present), and the acids. Make up to the 4 pints
(3 litres) mark with previously boiled water.
Leave for twenty-four hours at room
temperature, with frequent stirring.

(d) Dried fruit, by putting it through a mincing
machine and then proceeding as for jam, but
using Rohament P and Pectolase (if pectin is
present).

4   Make up to the 6 pints (4 litres) mark with
cool, previously boiled water. Take a
hydrometer reading at 21°C (70°F) if the main
ingredients contain sugar – adjust the sugar
content as necessary, using the Alcoholic
Strength Chart for 17% wines. Dissolve the
sugar in the minimum amount of water, or in
a little of the must which has been brought
briefly to the boil and then cooled to 21°C.
Stir in the grape tannin, ammonium phosphate,
and the yeast. If a yeast starter is being used,
this will have been prepared forty-eight hours
previously. Cover with a linen sheet to let the
air in and to keep the vinegar fly out.

5   Leave for four days, keeping a steady
temperature of 21°C (70°F) for white wines,
and 24°C (75°F) for rich red wines. These are
maximum temperatures, and a steady living
room temperature will serve to keep the yeast
active in its work. Stir three times each day.

6   Now syphon into a fermentation jar, and fit the airlock. Keep at 18°C (64°F) or room heat.

7   After three days (or specific gravity 1010), funnel in 1 pint (0.5 litre) of sugar solution, made with 13 fl oz (400 cc) of boiling water and ¾ lb (375 grammes) of sugar, which has been left to cool to 18°C before use.

8   After a further three days, repeat stage 7, using the last of the sugar and topping up with cool, previously boiled water to the neck of the fermentation jar, if such topping up is necessary.

9   Rack after seven days, discharging the syphon tube into a funnel in the sterile fermentation jar, so that a cascade occurs. This is the opposite procedure to that required for all wines except dessert wines. Top up with cool, boiled water.

10   Repeat stage 9, but after fourteen days.

11   Rack after a month, topping up as before.

12   Rack after a further month, topping up again.

13   Rack again after a month if fermentation has not ceased previously.
The fermentation lock can now be replaced by a small square of polythene wrapping material,

secured by a rubber band. Rack again if a deposit of sediment should occur, topping up as before.

14   Bottle, or syphon into bulk containers, all as previously described.

2 Jam Wines

Jams, Jellies, Purées, Conserves, and Marmalades Available

Apple
Apple and Blackcurrant
Apple and Plum
Apple and Raspberry
Apple and Strawberry
Apricot
Blackcurrant
Blueberry
Bramble
Cherry, Black
Cherry, Maraschino
Cherry, Morello
Cherry, Sweet
Cherry, Tart
Crabapple
Cranberry
Damson
Fig
Ginger
Golliberry
Gooseberry

Grape, Black
Grapefruit
Greengage
Lemon
Lime
Lime and Lemon
Loganberry
Mixed Fruit
Orange
Orange and Ginger
Peach
Pineapple
Plum, Red
Plum, Victoria
Quince
Raspberry
Raspberry, Seedless
Redcurrant
Rhubarb and Ginger
Strawberry

Basic Formulations

Aperitif Wines
Jam   4 lb (2.000 kg)
Sugar $\frac{1}{4}$ lb (125 g)

Tannin, grape   ½ tsp
Citric acid   ⅛ tsp (1.0 g)
Malic acid   ¼ tsp (1.5 g)
Tartaric acid   ¼ tsp (1.5 g)
Amm. phosphate 1 tsp (6.0 g)
Pectolase   ½ tsp
Yeast   1 tablet
Water   1 gallon (5.000 litres)
Lactose   1 oz (30.0 g)

Table Wines
Jam   3½ lb (1.750 kg)
Sugar   — (in jam)
Tannin, grape   ½ tsp
Citric acid   ⅛ tsp (1.0 g)
Malic acid   ¼ tsp (1.5 g)
Tartaric acid   ¼ tsp (1.5 g)
Amm. phosphate 1 tsp (6.0 g)
Pectolase   ½ tsp
Yeast   1 tablet
Water   1 gallon (5 litres)

Sparkling Table Wines
Jam   4 lb (2.000 kg)
Sugar   — (in jam)
Tannin, grape   ½ tsp
Citric acid   ⅛ tsp (1.0 g)
Malic acid   ¼ tsp (1.5 g)
Tartaric acid   ¼ tsp (1.5 g)
Amm. phosphate 1 tsp (6.0 g)
Pectolase   ½ tsp
Yeast   1 tablet
Water   1 gallon (5 litres)
Lactose   1 oz (30 g)

Social Wines

Jam	4½ lb (2.250 kg)
Sugar	— (in jam)
Tannin, grape	¾ tsp
Citric acid	¼ tsp (1.5 g)
Malic acid	½ tsp (3.0 g)
Tartaric acid	½ tsp (3.0 g)
Amm. phosphate	1 tsp (6.0 g)
Pectolase	1 tsp
Yeast	1 tablet
Water	1 gallon (5 litres)
Lactose	1½ oz (45 g)

Dessert Wines

Jam	5½ lb (2.750 kg)
Sugar	— (in jam)
Tannin, grape	1 tsp
Citric acid	¼ tsp (1.5 g)
Malic acid	½ tsp (3.0 g)
Tartaric acid	½ tsp (3.0 g)
Amm. phosphate	1 tsp (6.0 g)
Pectolase	1 tsp
Yeast	1 tablet
Water	1 gallon (5 litres)
Lactose	3 oz (90 g)

Home-made jams should not require the
addition of sugar – check with your
hydrometer. Fermentable sugar may have to be
provided with commercial jams – again check
with your hydrometer and the Alcoholic
Strength Chart. Citric acid will have been
added in the home-made jam, if needed, and
all three acids may be found in commercial
jams; add rather less than the given amounts.

RECIPES
Apple and Raspberry – dessert wine

Ingredients

Jam	5½ lb (2.750 kg)
Sugar	— (in jam)
Tannin, grape	1 tsp
Citric acid	¼ tsp (1.5 g)
Malic acid	½ tsp (3.0 g)
Tartaric acid	½ tsp (3.0 g)
Amm. phosphate	1 tsp (6.0 g)
Pectolase	1 tsp
Yeast, Madeira	1 Tablet
Water	1 gallon (5 litres)
Lactose	3 oz (90 g)

Method

Pour 4 pints (3 litres) of boiling water over
3 lb (1.5 kg) of the jam contained in a plastic
bucket. Cover, and when the must is at room
temperature, add half the Pectolase and half
the acids. Keep at room temperature, with
frequent stirring, for twenty-four hours.
Then heat up in a boiler and maintain briefly
at boiling point. Strain through a filter bag into
a bucket while still hot, and make up to the
6 pint (4 litre) mark with cool, previously
boiled water. Take a hydrometer reading when
the must has cooled to 21°C (70°F), and
with the aid of the Alcholoic Strength Chart
for 17% wines, add any required weight of
sugar in solution – use a little of the must in
which to dissolve the sugar. Stir in the grape
tannin, ammonium phosphate, and yeast;
a yeast starter should have been prepared

forty-eight hours previously if you are using this method. Cover the vessel with a square of linen sheeting. Leave for four days, keeping at 21°C (70°F) and stirring three times a day. Syphon into a fermentation jar, fit airlock, and keep at 18°C (64°F) for three days. On the second day, pour 1 pint (0.5 litre) of boiling water over 1¼ lb (0.625 kg) of the remaining untreated jam contained in another plastic bucket, cover and when at room temperature add half the remaining Pectolase and acids. Keep this must at room temperature for twenty-four hours, with frequent stirring, then heat up in a boiler briefly to boiling point. Strain and press out into another bucket and when cooled to 18°C (64°F), pour it into the fermentation jar which contains the first fermentation. The fermentation is allowed to proceed for a further three days. On the second day the remaining 1¼ lb (0.625 kg) of jam is prepared, as just described, for addition to the fermentation jar on the next day. Top up to the neck of the fermentation jar with cool, previously boiled water, if this level has not been reached. Rack after seven days, fourteen days, a month, a month, and a further month if a sediment shows itself. Finally bottle the wine as previously described, adding the lactose, dissolved in a little of the wine, at bottling, or decanting time.

Apple and Strawberry – social wine

Ingredients

Jam	4½ lb (2.250 kg)
Sugar	— (in jam)
Tannin, grape	¾ tsp
Citric acid	¼ tsp (1.5 g)
Malic acid	½ tsp (3.0 g)
Tartaric acid	½ tsp (3.0 g)
Amm. phosphate	1 tsp (6.0 g)
Pectolase	1 tsp
Rohament P	1 tsp
Yeast, GP	1 tablet
Water	1 gallon (5 litres)
Lactose	1½ oz (45 g)

Method

Pour 4 pints (3 litres) of boiling water onto the
jam contained in a plastic bucket, cover, and
allow to cool to room temperature. Add the
Rohament P, Pectolase and the acids, and
leave at room temperature, with frequent
stirring, for twenty-four hours. Then heat up in
a boiler, maintain briefly at boiling point, and
strain through a filter bag while still hot.
Cover with a sheet of linen and leave to cool
to 21°C (70°F). Make up to the gallon (5 litre)
mark with boiled and cooled water, and take a
hydrometer reading. Adjust the sugar content,
if necessary, using the Alcoholic Strength
Chart. Dissolve the sugar in the minimum
amount of water, or in a little of the must
brought briefly to the boil and then cooled to
21°C (70°F). If a yeast starter is being used,
this should have been prepared forty-eight

hours previously. Stir in the tannin, ammonium
phosphate and the yeast. Cover with a linen
sheet and leave for seven days at 21°C (70°F),
stirring three times a day. Syphon into a
fermentation jar, topping up to the neck with
boiled and cooled water if this level has not
been reached. Fit a fermentation lock, and
keep at 18°C (64°F) for a month, after which,
rack and top up. Rack and top up again at
monthly intervals until there is no more
sediment forming at the bottom of the jar.
Bottle after a total winemaking time of six
months, adding the lactose, dissolved in a
little of the wine, at bottling or decanting time.

Blackcurrant – dessert wine

Ingredients

Jam	5½ lb (2.750 kg)
Sugar	— (in jam)
Tannin, grape	1 tsp
Citric acid	¼ tsp (1.5 g)
Malic acid	½ tsp (3.0 g)
Tartaric acid	½ tsp (3.0 g)
Amm. phosphate	1 tsp (6.0 g)
Pectolase	1 tsp
Rohament P	1 tsp
Yeast, Port	1 tablet
Water	1 gallon (5 litres)
Lactose	3 oz (90 g)

Method

This is the same as for apple and raspberry
wine, except that the Rohament P, an
additional ingredient used to obtain maximum

extraction of flavour and colour from the
blackcurrants, is used at the same time and in
the same amount as the Pectolase; i.e. $\frac{1}{2}$ a
teaspoonful the first time, and a $\frac{1}{4}$ teaspoonful
on each of the two subsequent occasions.

Damson, Stoneless – aperitif wine

Ingredients

Jam	4 lb (2.000 kg)
Sugar	$\frac{1}{4}$ lb (125 g)
Citric acid	$\frac{1}{8}$ tsp (1.0 g)
Malic acid	$\frac{1}{4}$ tsp (1.5 g)
Tartaric acid	$\frac{1}{4}$ tsp (1.5 g)
Amm. phosphate	1 tsp (6.0 g)
Pectolase	$\frac{1}{2}$ tsp
Rohament P	$\frac{1}{2}$ tsp
Yeast, Sherry	1 tablet
Water	1 gallon (5 litres)
Lactose	1 oz (30 g)

Method
Pour 4 pints (3 litres) of boiling water onto the
jam contained in a plastic bucket, cover, and
allow it to cool to room temperature. Add the
Rohament P, Pectolase, and the acids, and
leave at room temperature, with frequent
stirring, for twenty-four hours. Then heat up
in a boiler, and maintain briefly at boiling
point. Strain through a filter bag while still hot.
Cover with a sheet of linen, and leave to cool
to 24°C (75°F). Make up to the gallon (5 litre)
mark with boiled and cooled water, and take a
hydrometer reading. Adjust the sugar content,
if necessary, using the Alcholic Strength

Chart. Dissolve the sugar in a little of the must transferred to a boiling pan; bring briefly to the boil, and then cool to 24°C (75°F). If a yeast starter is being used, this should have been prepared forty-eight hours previously. Stir in the ammonium phosphate and the yeast. Cover with a linen sheet, and leave for seven days at 24°C (75°F), stirring thrice daily.

Syphon into a fermentation jar, topping up to the neck with boiled and cooled water if this level has not been reached. Fit a fermentation lock, and keep at 18°C (64°F) for a month, after which, rack and top up. Rack and top up again at monthly intervals until there is no more sediment forming at the bottom of the jar. Bottle after a total winemaking time of six months, adding the lactose, dissolved in a little of the wine, at bottling or decanting time.

Gooseberry – sparkling table wine

Ingredients

Jam	4 lb (2.000 kg)
Sugar	— (in jam)
Tannin, grape	$\frac{1}{2}$ tsp
Citric acid	$\frac{1}{8}$ tsp (1.0 g)
Malic acid	$\frac{1}{4}$ tsp (1.5 g)
Tartaric acid	$\frac{1}{4}$ tsp (1.5 g)
Amm. phosphate	1 tsp (6.0 g)
Pectolase	$\frac{1}{2}$ tsp
Rohament P	$\frac{1}{2}$ tsp
Yeast, Champagne	1 tablet

Water   1 gallon (5 litres)
Lactose   1 oz (30 g)

Method
Pour 4 pints (3 litres) of boiling water onto the
jam contained in a plastic bucket, cover,
and allow to cool to room temperature. Add
the Rohament P, Pectolase and the acids, and
leave at room temperature, with frequent
stirring, for twenty-four hours. Then heat up
in a boiler, and maintain briefly at boiling
point. Strain through a filter bag while still hot.
Cover with a sheet of linen, and leave to cool
to 21°C (70°F). Make up to the gallon (5 litre)
mark with boiled and cooled water, and take
a hydrometer reading. Adjust the sugar
content if necessary, using the Alcoholic
Strength Chart. Dissolve the sugar in a little
of the must taken from the bucket, bring
briefly to the boil, and then cool to 21°C (70°F).
If a yeast starter is being used, this should have
been prepared forty-eight hours previously.
Stir in the tannin, ammonium phosphate, and
the yeast. Cover with the linen sheet, and leave
for five days at 21°C (70°F), stirring thrice
daily. Syphon into a fermentation jar, topping
up to the neck with boiled and cooled water if
this level has not been reached. Fit a
fermentation lock, and keep at 18°C (64°F) for
a month, after which, rack, top up, and save
some of the sedimentary yeast in the
refrigerator, as has been described. Rack and
top up again at monthly intervals, until there is
no more sediment forming at the bottom of
the jar. Bottle after a total winemaking time of

six months, all as previously described.
Make a yeast starter with your refrigerated
yeast at least three days before bottling, and
add a teaspoonful of sugar and a teaspoonful
of yeast starter to each champagne bottle,
together with the lactose dissolved in a little
of the wine.

Loganberry – social wine

Ingredients

Jam	4½ lb (2.250 kg)
Sugar	— (in jam)
Tannin, grape	¾ tsp
Citric acid	¼ tsp (1.5 g)
Malic acid	½ tsp (3.0 g)
Tartaric acid	½ tsp (3.0 g)
Amm. phosphate	1 tsp (6.0 g)
Pectolase	1 tsp
Yeast, Burgundy	1 tablet
Water	1 gallon (5 litres)
Lactose	1½ oz (45 g)

Method

This is the same as for apple and strawberry
wine, except that we don't need to use any
Rohament P.

Plum, Victoria – aperitif wine

Ingredients

Jam	4 lb (2.000 kg)
Sugar	¼ lb (125 g)
Citric acid	⅛ tsp (1.0 g)
Malic acid	¼ tsp (1.5 g)

Tartaric acid	¼ tsp (1.5 g)
Amm. phosphate	1 tsp (6.0 g)
Pectolase	½ tsp
Rohament P	½ tsp
Yeast, Sherry	1 tablet
Water	1 gallon (5 litres)
Lactose	1 oz (30 g)

Method
This is exactly the same as that described for damson wine, but you'll notice a difference when you come to taste the end product.

Quince – table wine

Ingredients

Jam	3½ lb (1.750 kg)
Sugar	— (in jam)
Tannin, grape	½ tsp
Citric acid	⅛ tsp (1.0 g)
Malic acid	¼ tsp (1.5 g)
Tartaric acid	¼ tsp (1.5 g)
Amm. phosphate	1 tsp (6.0 g)
Pectolase	½ tsp
Yeast, Burgundy	1 tablet
Water	1 gallon (5 litres)

Method
This is the same as for gooseberry wine, except that after the addition of the yeast the fermentation is allowed to proceed for three days only before syphoning into the fermentation jar. Furthermore, bottling does not include the addition of yeast or the use of champagne bottles.

Redcurrant – table wine

Ingredients

Jelly	3½ lb (1.750 kg)
Sugar	— (in jelly)
Tannin, grape	½ tsp
Citric acid	⅛ tsp (1.0 g)
Malic acid	¼ tsp (1.5 g)
Tartaric acid	¼ tsp (1.5 g)
Amm. phosphate	1 tsp (6.0 g)
Pectolase	½ tsp
Yeast, Madeira	1 tablet
Water	1 gallon (5 litres)

Method

This again is the same as for gooseberry wine, except that after the addition of the yeast the fermentation is allowed to proceed for three days only, before syphoning into the fermentation jar; furthermore, bottling does not include the addition of yeast or the use of champagne bottles. This is a rosé wine, and the fermentation jar should be protected from natural light before the wine is syphoned into dark coloured bottles. ·

3 Canned Fruit Wines

Fruits Available

Canned

Apple	Mango
Apricot	Melon
Blackberry	Orange, Mandarin
Blackcurrant	Paw-paw
Cherry, Black	Peach
Cherry, Morello	Pear
Damson	Pineapple
Fig	Plum, Golden
Fruit Cocktail	Plum, Red
Fruit Salad	Plum, Victoria
Gooseberry	Prune
Grapefruit	Raspberry
Greengage	Redcurrant
Guava	Rhubarb
Loganberry	Strawberry
Lichee	

Pie and Flan Fillings	*Juices*
Apple	Apple
Apple and Blackberry	Blackcurrant
Apple and Blackcurrant	Cherry
Apricot	Grape, Red
Bilberry	Grape, White
Blackcurrant	Grapefruit
Cherry	Lemon
Gooseberry	Orange
Lemon	Pineapple

Lime	Raspberry
Orange	Ribena
Peach	Rosehip
Pineapple	Rosehip and
Raspberry	Orange
Rhubarb	Tangerine
Strawberry	

Basic Formulations

Aperitif Wines

Fruit, canned	1¾ lb (0.875 kg)
Sugar	2½ lb (1.250 kg)
Tannin, grape	½ tsp
Citric acid	¼ tsp (1.5 g)
Malic acid	½ tsp (3.0 g)
Tartaric acid	½ tsp (3.0 g)
Amm. phosphate	1 tsp (6.0 g)
Rohament P	½ tsp
Yeast	1 tablet
Water	1 gallon (5 litres)
Lactose	1 oz (30 g)

Table Wines

Fruit, canned	1¼ lb (0.625 kg)
Sugar	1¾ lb (0.875 kg)
Tannin, grape	½ tsp
Citric acid	¼ tsp (1.5 g)
Malic acid	½ tsp (3.0 g)
Tartaric acid	½ tsp (3.0 g)
Amm. phosphate	1 tsp (6.0 g)
Rohament P	½ tsp
Yeast	1 tablet
Water	1 gallon (5 litres)

Sparkling Table Wines

Fruit, canned	1¾ lb (0.875 kg)
Sugar	2¼ lb (1.125 kg)
Tannin, grape	½ tsp
Citric acid	¼ tsp (1.5 g)
Malic acid	½ tsp (3.0 g)
Tartaric acid	½ tsp (3.0 g)
Amm. phosphate	1 tsp (6.0 g)
Rohament P	½ tsp
Yeast	1 tablet
Water	1 gallon (5 litres)
Lactose	1 oz (30.0 g)

Social Wines

Fruit, canned	2¼ lb (1.125 kg)
Sugar	2½ lb (1.250 kg)
Tannin, grape	1 tsp
Citric acid	¼ tsp (1.5 g)
Malic acid	¾ tsp (4.0 g)
Tartaric acid	¾ tsp (4.0 g)
Amm. phosphate	1 tsp (6.0 g)
Rohament P	½ tsp
Yeast	1 tablet
Water	1 gallon (5 litres)
Lactose	1½ oz (45.0 g)

Dessert Wines

Fruit, canned	3¼ lb (1.625 kg)
Sugar	3 lb (1.500 kg)
Tannin, grape	1 tsp
Citric acid	½ tsp (2.5 g)
Malic acid	1 tsp (5.0 g)
Tartaric acid	1 tsp (5.0 g)
Amm. phosphate	1 tsp (6.0 g)
Rohament P	1 tsp

Yeast   1 tablet
Water   1 gallon (5 litres)
Lactose   3 oz (90.0 g)

RECIPES
Blackberry – dessert wine

Ingredients
Blackberries, canned $3\frac{1}{4}$ lb (1.625 kg)
Sugar $2\frac{3}{4}$ lb (1.375 kg)
Tannin, grape   1 tsp
Citric acid   1 tsp (6.0 g)
Tartaric acid $1\frac{1}{2}$ tsp (9.0 g)
Amm. phosphate   1 tsp (6.0 g)
Yeast, Port   1 tablet
Rohament P   1 tsp
Water   1 gallon (5 litres)
Lactose $1\frac{1}{2}$ oz (45.0 g)

Method
Pour the contents of the tin into a plastic
bucket, and pulp with a stainless steel potato
masher. Add 4 pints (3 litres) of previously
boiled water cooled to room temperature,
stir in the acids and the Rohament P and
leave covered for twenty-four hours, with
frequent stirring. Heat up briefly to boiling
point in a boiler and strain through a filter bag
back into the bucket, squeezing out while still
hot as much juice as possible from the solids
left in the filter bag. Cover with a square of
linen and leave to cool. Make up to the 6 pint
(4 litre) mark with cool, previously boiled
water. Take a hydrometer reading at 21°C
(70°F), and adjust the sugar content as

necessary, using the Alcoholic Strength Chart
for 17% wines. Dissolve the sugar in a little
of the must which is brought briefly to the
boil, and leave to cool to 21°C. Stir in the
grape tannin, ammonium phosphate, and the
yeast. If a yeast starter is being used, this
should have been prepared forty-eight hours
previously. Cover with a square of linen, and
leave for four days at 24°C (75°F), stirring
thrice daily. Syphon into a fermentation jar, fit
the airlock, and keep at 18°C (64°F) for a
further three days. Now funnel into the jar
1 pint (0.5 litres) of sugar solution, made with
13 fl oz (400 ccs) of boiling water in which ¾ lb
(375 grammes) of sugar has been dissolved
and the syrup allowed to cool; refit the
airlock. After a further three days, repeat this
operation with the remainder of the sugar,
and top up with cool, previously boiled water
to the neck of the jar, if this level has not been
reached. Rack after seven more days, topping
up as necessary, and refitting the airlock.
Rack again after a further fourteen days, and
at monthly intervals thereafter, until there is
no further sedimentation. Bottle after a total
winemaking time of six months, adding the
lactose in solution, and store at 7–10°C
(45–50°F).

Cherry, Black – table wine

Ingredients

Cherries, canned	1¼ lb (0.625 kg)
Sugar	1¾ lb (0.875 kg)
Citric acid	¼ tsp (1.5 g)

Tartaric acid	½ tsp (3.0 g)
Amm. phosphate	1 tsp (6.0 g)
Rohament P	½ tsp
Yeast, Sherry	1 tablet
Water	1 gallon (5 litres)

Method
Pour out the canned black cherries into a
plastic bucket, and pulp with a stainless steel
potato masher. Add 4 pints (3 litres) of
previously boiled water cooled to room
temperature, together with the Rohament P
and the acids. Leave at this temperature,
with frequent stirring, and covered with a
sheet of linen for twenty-four hours. Pour out
into a boiler, and heat up to and maintain
briefly at boiling point. Then pour through a
filter bag back into the bucket, and squeeze
out as much juice as possible while still hot.
Cover with a sheet of linen, and when cool
make up to the gallon (5 litre) mark with
previously boiled and cooled water. Take a
hydrometer reading at 21°C (70°F), and adjust
the sugar content as necessary with the aid
of the Alcoholic Strength Chart. Dissolve the
required weight of sugar (about 1¾ lb) (875
grammes) in a little of the must brought
briefly to the boil, and cool to 21°C before
returning to the bucket. Stir in the ammonium
phosphate and the yeast. If a yeast starter is
being used, this should have been prepared
forty-eight hours previously. Cover with the
sheet of linen, and leave at 21°C (70°F) for
three days, stirring thrice daily. Syphon into
a fermentation jar, topping up to the neck

with boiled and cooled water if this level has not been reached. Fit an airlock, and keep at 18° C (64°F), or room temperature, for a month. Rack, and top up with boiled and cooled water. Rack at monthly intervals so long as there is a sediment from which the young wine has to be removed, and top up as before, refitting the airlock. Bottle, or syphon into bulk containers, after a total winemaking time of six months, and store at 7–10°C (45–50°F).

This is a dry, sherry-type wine, and no lactose is needed unless your taste buds demand a sweet wine, when not more than 1 oz (30 grammes) of lactose in solution should be introduced.

Cherry, Morello – aperitif wine

Ingredients

Cherries, Morello	1¾ lb (0.875 kg)
Sugar	2½ lb (1.250 kg)
Citric acid	⅛ tsp (1.0 g)
Tartaric acid	¼ tsp (1.5 g)
Amm. phosphate	1 tsp (6.0 g)
Rohament P	½ tsp
Yeast, Champagne	1 tablet
Water	1 gallon (5 litres)

Method

Pour out the canned Morello cherries into a plastic bucket, and pulp with a stainless steel potato masher or similar utensil. Add 4 pints (3 litres) of previously boiled water cooled to room temperature, together with the Rohament

P and the acids. Do no exceed the given
amounts of these, since they are lower than
usual in view of the high natural acid content
of cherries. Leave at this temperature, with
frequent stirring, and covered with a square of
linen, for twenty-four hours. Pour out into a
boiler, and heat up briefly to boiling point.
Then pour through a filter bag back into the
bucket, and while still hot squeeze out as
much juice as possible. Cover with the square
of linen, and when cool make up to the
gallon (5 litre) mark with previously boiled and
cooled water. Take a hydrometer reading at
21°C (70°F) and adjust the sugar content, as
necessary, with the aid of the Alcoholic
Strength Chart for 14% wines. Dissolve the
required weight of sugar (about $2\frac{1}{2}$ lb) (1.25 kg)
in a little of the must brought briefly to the
boil, and cool to 21°C before returning to the
bucket. Stir in the ammonium phosphate and
the yeast. If a yeast starter is being used, this
should have been prepared forty-eight hours
previously. Cover with a sheet of linen and
leave at 21°C for seven days, stirring thrice daily.
Syphon into a fermentation jar, topping up
to the neck with boiled and cooled water if
this level has not been reached. Fit an airlock
and keep at 18°C (64°F), or room temperature,
for a month. Rack at monthly intervals so long
as a sediment forms. It would spoil the wine if
left in contact. Top up as previously
described, refitting the airlock. Bottle, or
syphon into bulk containers, after a total
winemaking time of six months, and store at
7–10°C (45–50°F).

Pear – sparkling table wine

Ingredients

Pears, canned	1¾ lb (0.875 kg)
Sugar	2¼ lb (1.125 kg)
Tannin, grape	½ tsp
Malic acid	½ tsp (3.0 g)
Tartaric acid	¾ tsp (4.5 g)
Amm. phosphate	1 tsp (6.0 g)
Rohament P	½ tsp
Yeast, Champagne	1 tablet
Water	1 gallon (5 litres)
Lactose	1 oz (30 g)

Method

This is the same as for canned black cherry table wine, except that tannin is added at the same time as the ammonium phosphate and the yeast. Furthermore, some of the yeast sediment obtained after the first racking from the fermentation jar (not from the bucket) is stored in the refrigerator, after which, it is started into fermentation, as described, at least three days before bottling time. A teaspoonful of this starter, and a teaspoonful of sugar, together with the lactose dissolved in a little of the wine, is added to each champagne bottle before the cork is wired down.

Raspberry – table wine

Ingredients

Raspberry, canned	1¼ lb (0.625 kg)
Sugar	1¾ lb (0.875 kg)
Tannin, grape	½ tsp

Amm. phosphate	1 tsp (6.0 g)
Rohament P	$\frac{1}{2}$ tsp
Yeast, Madeira	1 tablet
Water	1 gallon (5 litres)

Method
This is the same as for canned black cherries, but there are differences in some of the ingredients used. The tannin is added to the must at the same time as the yeast, together with the ammonium phosphate. There are no acids to be added, since this fruit is particularly strong in natural acid content.

Strawberry – social wine

Ingredients

Strawberries, canned	$2\frac{1}{4}$ lb (1.125 kg)
Sugar	$2\frac{1}{2}$ lb (1.250 kg)
Tannin, grape	1 tsp
Malic acid	$\frac{3}{4}$ tsp (4.5 g)
Tartaric acid	1 tsp (6.0 g)
Amm. phosphate	1 tsp (6.0 g)
Rohament P	$\frac{1}{2}$ tsp
Yeast, Sherry	1 tablet
Water	1 gallon (5 litres)
Lactose	$1\frac{1}{2}$ oz (45 g)

Method
This is the same as for canned black cherry table wine, except that grape tannin is added at the same time as the yeast and ammonium phosphate. The initial fermentation in the bucket is allowed to proceed for seven days and lactose is added at bottling time, as has been described.

4 Dried Fruit Wines

Dried Fruits Available

Apple	Date	Raisin, seedless
Apricot	Elderberry	Rosehip
Banana	Fig	Rosehip shells
Bilberry	Mixed fruit	Rowanberry
Candied peel	Peach	Sloe
Cherry	Prune	Sultana
Currant	Raisin	

Basic Formulations

Aperitif Wines

Dried Fruit	1¼ lb (0.625 kg)*
Sugar	2 lb (1.000 kg)*
Tannin, grape	½ tsp
Citric acid	¼ tsp (1.5 g)
Malic acid	½ tsp (3.0 g)
Tartaric acid	½ tsp (3.0 g)
Amm. phosphate	1 tsp (6.0 g)
Rohament P	1½ tsp
Yeast	1 tablet
Water	1 gallon (5 litres)
Lactose	1 oz (30.0 g)

* Use double the given amounts in all the
Basic Formulations of currants, raisins,
sultanas, dates and figs, and then double
the amount of Rohament P (and Pectolase if
used). At the same time, use half the weight

of sugar given, to allow for the additional
amount of natural sugar content introduced.
It is advisable to take a hydrometer reading in
all cases, and adjust the variable natural sugar
content accordingly.

Table Wines
Dried fruit	1 lb (0.500 kg)
Sugar	1¼ lb (0.625 kg)
Tannin, grape	½ tsp
Citric acid	¼ tsp (1.5 g)
Malic acid	½ tsp (3.0 g)
Tartaric acid	½ tsp (3.0 g)
Amm. phosphate	1 tsp (6.0 g)
Rohament P	1 tsp
Yeast	1 tablet
Water	1 gallon (5 litres)

Sparkling Table Wines
Dried fruit	1¼ lb (0.625 kg)
Sugar	1¾ lb (0.875 kg)
Tannin, grape	½ tsp
Citric acid	¼ tsp (1.5 g)
Malic acid	½ tsp (3.0 g)
Tartaric acid	½ tsp (3.0 g)
Amm. phosphate	1 tsp (6.0 g)
Rohament P	1½ tsp
Yeast	1 tablet
Water	1 gallon (5 litres)
Lactose	1 oz (30.0 g)

Social Wines
Dried fruit	1¼ lb (0.750 kg)
Sugar	1¾ lb (0.875 kg)
Tannin, grape	1 tsp

Citric acid	¼ tsp (1.5 g)
Malic acid	¾ tsp (4.0 g)
Tartaric acid	¾ tsp (4.0 g)
Amm. phosphate	1 tsp (6.0 g)
Rohament P	1½ tsp
Yeast	1 tablet
Water	1 gallon (5 litres)
Lactose	1½ oz (45.0 g)

Dessert Wines

Dried fruit	2 lb (1.000 kg)
Sugar	2 lb (1.000 kg)
Tannin, grape	1 tsp
Citric acid	½ tsp (3.0 g)
Malic acid	1 tsp (5.0 g)
Tartaric acid	1 tsp (5.0 g)
Amm. phosphate	1 tsp (6.0 g)
Rohament P	2 tsp
Yeast	1 tablet
Water	1 gallon (5 litres)
Lactose	3 oz (90.0 g)

RECIPES
Apple – aperitif wine

Ingredients

Apple, dried	1¼ lb (0.625 kg)
Sultanas	½ lb (0.250 kg)
Sugar	2¼ lb (1.125 kg)
Tannin, grape	½ tsp
Citric acid	½ tsp (3.0 g)
Tartaric acid	½ tsp (3.0 g)
Amm. phosphate	1 tsp (6.0 g)
Fungal amylase	¼ tsp (1.0 g)

Pectolase	2 tsp
Rohament P	2 tsp
Yeast, Champagne	1 tablet
Water	1 gallon (5 litres)

Method
If the dried fruit is not prepacked, put it into a
colander and rinse with cold, running water.
Put it through a mincing machine, and then
into a plastic bucket. Pour 4 pints (3 litres) of
boiling water over it, cover, and allow it to
cool to room temperature. Then add the
Rohament P, Pectolase, Fungal amylase, and
the acids. Leave at room temperature for
twenty-four hours, with frequent stirring. Pour
out into a boiler, and heat briefly to boiling
point. Strain through a filter bag and funnel
back into the bucket while still hot, pressing
out the remaining juice from the solids
contained in the filter bag. Cover with a sheet
of linen and leave to cool. Make up to the
gallon (5 litre) mark with boiled and cooled
water, and take a hydrometer reading at 21°C
(70°F) – you can now adjust the sugar content,
as necessary, with the aid of the Alcoholic
Strength Chart. Dissolve the sugar in a little
of the must brought briefly to the boil, and
cool to 21°C before adding to the contents of
the bucket. Stir in the grape tannin, ammonium
phosphate, and the yeast. If a yeast starter is
being used, this should have been prepared
forty-eight hours previously. Cover with a
sheet of linen, and keep at this temperature
or at room temperature for seven days,
stirring thrice daily. Then syphon into a

fermentation jar, topping up to the neck with
boiled and cooled water and fit the
fermentation lock. Keep at 18°C (64°F) for a
month. Then syphon off from the solids at the
bottom of the jar, top up, and refit the
fermentation lock. Rack at monthly intervals if
sedimentation continues to be thrown. Bottle,
or syphon into bulk storage containers after a
total winemaking time of six months, and store
at 7–10°C (45–50°F).

Banana – sparkling table wine

Ingredients

Banana, dried	1 lb (0.500 kg)
Sultanas	$\frac{1}{2}$ lb (0.250 kg)
Sugar	$2\frac{1}{4}$ lb (1.125 kg)
Tannin, grape	$\frac{1}{2}$ tsp
Tartaric acid	1 tsp (6.0 g)
Amm. phosphate	1 tsp (6.0 g)
Rohament P	$1\frac{1}{2}$ tsp
Yeast, Champagne	1 tablet
Water	1 gallon (5 litres)

Method

If the sultanas are not prepacked, put them in
a colander and rinse with cold, running water.
Put the dried fruit through a mincing machine
and then into a plastic bucket. Pour 4 pints
(3 litres) of boiling water over it, cover, and
leave it to cool to room temperature. Then add
the Rohament P and the acid. Leave at room
temperature for twenty-four hours, with
frequent stirring. Pour out into a boiler, heat
and maintain briefly at boiling point. Strain

through a filter bag, and funnel back into the bucket while still hot, pressing out the remaining juice from the solids contained in the filter bag. Cover with a sheet of linen and leave to cool. Make up to the gallon (5 litre) mark with boiled and cooled water, and take a hydrometer reading at 21°C (70°F). You can now adjust the sugar content, as necessary, with the aid of the Alcholic Strength Chart. Dissolve the sugar (you'll need about $2\frac{1}{4}$ lb – 1.125 kg) in a little of the must brought briefly to the boil, and allow it to cool to 21°C before adding to the contents of the bucket. Stir in the grape tannin, ammonium phosphate and yeast. If a yeast starter is being used, it should have been prepared forty-eight hours previously. Cover with a sheet of linen and keep at this temperature, or at room temperature for five days, stirring thrice daily. Then syphon into a fermentation jar, topping up to the neck with boiled and cooled water if this level has not been reached. Fit the fermentation lock and keep at 18°C (64°F) for a month. Then syphon off from the solids at the bottom of the jar, top up, and refit the fermentation lock. Save some of the yeast deposit in the refrigerator. Rack at monthly intervals if further sedimentation occurs. Bottle into champagne bottles after a total winemaking time of six months but, three days previous to bottling, make a yeast starter from the refrigerated yeast, adding a teaspoonful of this, and a teaspoonful of sugar dissolved in a little of the wine, to each bottle before wiring down.

Bilberry – dessert wine

Ingredients

Bilberries, dried	1 lb (0.500 kg)
Raisins	2 lb (1.000 kg)
Sugar	2 lb (1.000 kg)
Citric acid	½ tsp (3.0 g)
Malic acid	1 tsp (6.0 g)
Tartaric acid	1 tsp (6.0 g)
Amm. phosphate	1 tsp (6.0 g)
Rohament P	3 tsp
Yeast, Port	1 tablet
Water	1 gallon (5 litres)
Lactose	1½ oz (45.0 g)

Method

If the dried fruit is not prepacked, put it into a colander and rinse it well with cold, running water under the tap. Put it through a mincing machine and into a plastic bucket. Pour 4 pints (3 litres) of boiling water over it, cover with a square of linen sheeting and leave it to cool to room temperature. Then add the Rohament P and the acids, and keep at room temperature, with frequent stirring, for twenty-four hours. Transfer to a boiler, heat up, and maintain briefly at boiling point. Strain through a filter bag back into the bucket while still hot, pressing out the remaining juice from the solids. Cover with the square of linen and leave to cool. Make up to the 6 pint (4 litre) mark with cool, previously boiled water. Take a hydrometer reading at 21°C (70°F) and adjust the sugar content as necessary, using the Alcoholic Strength Chart for 17% wines.

Dissolve the sugar in a little of the must which has been brought briefly to the boil and cool to 21°C before adding to the contents of the bucket. You will now have 1½ lb (0.750 kg) of combined natural and household sugar in the must, and will need to add a further 1¾ lb (0.875 kg) of household sugar in two further stages, but for the present stir in the ammonium phosphate and the yeast. If a yeast starter is being used, this should have been prepared forty-eight hours previously. Cover with a square of linen and leave for four days, keeping a steady temperature of 24°C (75°F), and stirring thrice daily. Now syphon the must into a fermentation jar, fit an airlock, and keep at room temperature for three more days. Then pour in 1 pint (0.5 litres) of sugar solution. This should be made with 13 fl oz (400 ccs) of boiling water in which ¾ lb (375 grammes) of sugar has been dissolved. The syrup must be allowed to cool to room temperature before use. After a further three days, add the rest of the sugar solution, prepared as described. Top up to the neck of the fermentation jar with cool, previously boiled water, if this level has not been reached. Rack after seven days, discharging the syphon tube (a procedure used only in the case of dessert wines) into a funnel in the neck of the fermentation jar. Top up with cool, previously boiled water. Rack again after a further fourteen days. Repeat the racking thereafter at monthly intervals, so long as a sediment forms on the bottom of the jar. Bottle, or syphon into bulk storage

containers after a total winemaking time of
six months, adding the lactose, dissolved in a
little of the wine, at bottling or decanting
time. Store at 7–10°C (45–50°F). You will see
that we have used only half of the weight of
lactose given in the basic formulation for
dessert wines, for dessert port wine is
usually served, and best appreciated,
medium-sweet.

Cherry – sparkling table wine

Ingredients

Cherry, dried	1 lb (0.500 kg)
Sultanas	½ lb (0.250 kg)
Sugar	2¼ lb (1.125 kg)
Tannin, grape	½ tsp
Citric acid	½ tsp (3.0 g)
Tartaric acid	½ tsp (3.0 g)
Amm. phosphate	1 tsp (6.0 g)
Rohament P	1½ tsp
Yeast, Champagne	1 tablet
Water	1 gallon (5 litres)
Lactose	1 oz (30.0 g)

Method
This is the same as for dried banana
sparkling table wine, but lactose can be added
at the same time as the sugar, dissolved in a
little of the wine at bottling time, if a sweet
champagne is preferred to the dry type.

Currant – table wine

Ingredients

Currants	2 lb (1.000 kg)
Sugar	¾ lb (0.375 kg)
Citric acid	1 tsp (6.0 g)
Amm. phosphate	1 tsp (6.0 g)
Rohament P	2 tsp
Yeast, Sherry	1 tablet
Water	1 gallon (5 litres)

Method

If the dried fruit is not prepacked, put it into a colander, and rinse with cold, running water. Put it through a mincing machine, and then into a plastic bucket. Pour 4 pints (3 litres) of boiling water over it, cover and leave it to cool to room temperature, then add the Rohament P and the acid. Leave at room temperature for twenty-four hours, with frequent stirring. Pour out into a boiler, heat and maintain briefly at boiling point. Strain through a filter bag, and funnel back into the bucket while still hot, pressing out the remaining juice from the solids. Cover with a sheet of linen, and leave to cool. Make up to the gallon (5 litre) mark with boiled and cooled water, and take a hydrometer reading at 21°C (70°F). You can now adjust the sugar content as necessary, with the aid of the Alcoholic Strength Chart. Dissolve the sugar (you'll need about ¾ lb – 0.375 kg) in a little of the must brought briefly to the boil, and cool it to 21°C before adding to the contents of the bucket. Stir in the ammonium phosphate and the yeast. If a yeast starter is being used, it should have been prepared forty-eight hours previously. Cover with a sheet of linen and keep at this temperature, or at room temperature, for three days, stirring thrice daily. Then syphon into a fermentation jar, topping up to the neck with boiled and cooled water and fit the fermentation lock. Keep at 18°C (64°F) for a month. Then syphon off from the solids at the bottom of the jar, and top up, refitting the airlock. Rack at monthly intervals if further sedimentation occurs. Bottle, or syphon into bulk storage containers after a total winemaking time of six months, and store at 7–10°C (45–50°F). Bulk storage containers are appropriate for all table wines, which are imbibed in greater quantities than other wines except perhaps, social wines.

Date – table wine

Ingredients

Dates	2 lb (1.000 kg)
Sugar	$\frac{3}{4}$ lb (0.375 kg)
Tannin, grape	$\frac{1}{2}$ tsp
Citric acid	$\frac{1}{4}$ tsp (1.5 g)
Malic acid	$\frac{1}{2}$ tsp (3.0 g)
Tartaric acid	$\frac{1}{2}$ tsp (3.0 g)
Amm. phosphate	1 tsp (6.0 g)
Rohament P	2 tsp
Yeast, Sherry	1 tablet
Water	1 gallon (5 litres)

Method
This is the same as for currant table wine.
The malic and tartaric acids are added at the
same time as the citric acid and Rohament P.
The tannin is added at the same time as the
ammonium phosphate and the yeast. If you do
not appreciate dry sherry wines you can add
1 oz (30 grammes) of lactose at bottling time,
but sweet sherry is more generally favoured
for social and dessert wines.

Elderberry – dessert wine

Ingredients

Elderberries, dried	1 lb (0.500 kg)
Raisins	2 lb (1.000 kg)
Sugar	2 lb (1.000 kg)
Citric acid	½ tsp (3.0 g)
Malic acid	1 tsp (6.0 g)
Tartaric acid	1 tsp (6.0 g)
Amm. phosphate	1 tsp (6.0 g)
Rohament P	3 tsp
Yeast, Port	1 tablet
Water	1 gallon (5 litres)
Lactose	1½ oz (45.0 g)

Method
This is the same as for dried bilberry dessert
wine. You will note that, owing to the natural
sugar content of the dried fruit, your
hydrometer will indicate that only about ¼ lb
(125 grammes) of household sugar is required
before the addition of the yeast. When the
yeast has converted this sugar, together with
the natural sugar content, into alcohol, then

the remaining 1¾ lb (875 grammes) of household sugar is added, in solution as syrup, in two stages. Since the total sugar requirement in our formulation is 3¼ lb (1.625 kg) you will readily deduce that the natural sugar content will be 1¼ lb (0.625 kg) in 6 pints (4 litres) of must. The hydrometer may well indicate a concentration of 1½ lb (750 grammes) of sugar (S.G. 1.072), in which case no household sugar should be added until after the four days of fermentation in the bucket, followed by the three days of fermentation in the fermentation jar. Then the amount to be added in two stages will be the same as before – 1¾ lb (875 grammes).

Fig – sparkling table wine

Ingredients

Figs, dried	2½ lb (1.250 kg)
Sugar	1¼ lb (0.625 kg)
Tannin, grape	½ tsp
Malic acid	½ tsp (3.0 g)
Tartaric acid	1 tsp (6.0 g)
Amm. phosphate	1 tsp (6.0 g)
Rohament P	2½ tsp
Yeast, Champagne	1 tablet
Water	1 gallon (5 litres)

Method

This is the same as for dried banana sparkling table wine.

Mixed Fruit – aperitif wine

Ingredients

Mixed dried fruit	$2\frac{1}{2}$ lb (1.250 kg)
Sugar	2 lb (1.000 kg)
Tannin, grape	$\frac{1}{2}$ tsp
Citric acid	$\frac{1}{4}$ tsp (1.5 g)
Malic acid	$\frac{1}{2}$ tsp (3.0 g)
Tartaric acid	$\frac{1}{2}$ tsp (3.0 g)
Amm. phosphate	1 tsp (6.0 g)
Pectolase	$2\frac{1}{2}$ tsp
Rohament P	$2\frac{1}{2}$ tsp
Yeast, Madeira	1 tablet
Water	1 gallon (5 litres)

Method

This is the same as for dried apple aperitif
wine. You may have noticed that lactose is not
mentioned for either of these wines. This is
because a Madeira wine is usually more
acceptable as a dry aperitif. If your preference
is for a sweet wine, add 1 oz (30 grammes)
of lactose dissolved in a little of the wine at
bottling or decanting time.

Peach – social wine

Ingredients

Peaches, dried	1 lb (0.500 kg)
Sultanas	1 lb (0.500 kg)
Sugar	$1\frac{3}{4}$ lb (0.875 kg)
Citric acid	1 tsp (6.0 g)
Tartaric acid	1 tsp (6.0 g)
Amm. phosphate	1 tsp (6.0 g)

Pectolase	2 tsp
Rohament P	2 tsp
Yeast, Sauterne	1 tablet
Water	1 gallon (5 litres)
Lactose	$1\frac{1}{2}$ oz (45.0 g)

Method

If the dried fruit is not prepacked, put it into a
colander and rinse with cold, running water.
Put it through a mincing machine and then
into a plastic bucket. Pour 4 pints (3 litres)
of boiling water over it, cover and leave it to
cool to room temperature. Then add the
Pectolase, Rohament P and the acids. Leave at
room temperature for twenty-four hours, with
frequent stirring. Pour out into a boiler, heat
and maintain briefly at boiling point. Strain
through a filter bag, and funnel back into the
bucket while still hot, pressing out the
remaining juice from the solids. Cover with
a sheet of linen and leave to cool. Make up to
the gallon (5 litre) mark with boiled and cooled
water, and take a hydrometer reading at 21°C
(70°F). You can now adjust the sugar content,
as necessary, with the aid of the Alcoholic
Strength Chart. Dissolve the sugar (you'll
need about $1\frac{3}{4}$ lb – 0.875 kg) in a little of the
must brought briefly to the boil, and cooled
to 21°C before adding it to the contents of the
bucket. Stir in the ammonium phosphate and
the yeast. If a yeast starter is being used, this
should have been prepared forty-eight hours
previously. Cover with a sheet of linen, and
keep at this temperature, or at room
temperature, for seven days, stirring thrice

daily. Then syphon into a fermentation jar,
topping up to the neck with boiled and cooled
water and fit a fermentation lock. Keep at 18°C
(64°F) for a month. Then syphon off from the
solids at the bottom of the jar, and top up,
refitting the airlock. Rack at monthly intervals
until no further sedimentation occurs. Bottle,
or syphon into bulk storage containers after
a total winemaking time of six months, and
store at 7–10°C (45–50°F). The lactose
required to give a sweet wine is dissolved in a
litttle of the wine at bottling or at decanting
time, and added to the bulk.

Prune – dessert wine

Ingredients

Prunes	2 lb (1.000 kg)
Sugar	2½ lb (1.250 kg)
Tannin, grape	1 tsp
Citric acid	1 tsp (6.0 g)
Tartaric acid	1 tsp (6.0 g)
Amm. phosphate	1 tsp (6.0 g)
Pectolase	2 tsp
Rohament P	2 tsp
Yeast, Madeira	1 tablet.
Water	1 gallon (5 litres)
Lactose	3 oz (90.0 g)

Method

This is the same as for dried bilberry dessert
wine, but tannin and Pectolase are used here
and malic acid is omitted. The Pectolase is
added at the same time as the Rohament P,
and the tannln with the yeast. The full amount

of lactose specified in the basic formulation
for dessert wines is used, since this is a
full-bodied and robust sweet Madeira wine.

Raisin (Seedless) – social wine

Ingredients

Raisins	3 lb (1.500 kg)
Sugar	¾ lb (0.375 kg)
Citric acid	¼ tsp (1.5 g)
Amm. phosphate	1 tsp (6.0 g)
Rohament P	3 tsp
Yeast, Sherry	1 tablet
Water	1 gallon (5 litres)
Lactose	1½ oz (45.0 g)

Method

This is the same as for dried peach social
wine, except that Pectolase is not required.

Rosehip (Shells) – dessert wine

Ingredients

Rose hip shells	¾ lb (0.375 kg)
Raisins	2½ lb (1.250 kg)
Sugar	1¾ lb (0.875 kg)
Citric acid	½ tsp (3.0 g)
Malic acid	1 tsp (6.0 g)
Tartaric acid	1 tsp (6.0 g)
Amm. phosphate	1 tsp (6.0 g)
Rohament P	3 tsp
Yeast, Sherry	1 tablet
Water	1 gallon (5 litres)
Lactose	3 oz (90.0 g)

Method

This is the same as for dried bilberry dessert wine, except that the extra natural sugar content must be allowed for. The hydrometer reading at 21°C (70°F) may well be 1.086, indicating the presence of 1 lb 10 oz (810 grammes) of sugar in 6 pints (4 litres) of must. The total weight of natural and household sugar must be $3\frac{1}{4}$ lb (1.625 kg) which means that we have to add 1 lb 10 oz (810 grammes) of household sugar in two doses of 13 oz (405 grammes) each, dissolved in water as has been described.

Sloe – social wine

Ingredients

Sloes, dried	1 lb (0.500 kg)
Raisins	1 lb (0.500 kg)
Sugar	$2\frac{1}{4}$ lb (1.125 kg)
Tannin, grape	$\frac{1}{2}$ tsp
Citric acid	$\frac{1}{4}$ tsp (1.5 g)
Malic acid	$\frac{3}{4}$ tsp (4.5 g)
Tartaric acid	$\frac{3}{4}$ tsp (4.5 g)
Amm. phosphate	1 tsp (6.0 g)
Pectolase	2 tsp
Rohament P	2 tsp
Yeast, Burgundy	1 tablet
Water	1 gallon (5 litres)

Method

This is the same as for dried peach social wine, except that some tannin is supplied by the sloes, so we cut down the grape tannin to half that given in the basic formulation for

dried fruit social wines and use it at the same
time as the yeast. You will note that lactose
has not been included in our formulation, since
a dry Burgundy-type wine is more generally
favoured for social occasions.

Sultana – table wine

Ingredients

Sultanas	2 lb (1.000 kg)
Bananas, dried	½ lb (0.250 kg)
Sugar	¾ lb (0.375 kg)
Citric acid	1 tsp (6.0 g)
Amm. phosphate	1 tsp (6.0 g)
Rohament P	3 tsp
Yeast, Graves	1 tablet
Water	1 gallon (5 litres)

Method

This is the same as for currant table wine, the
bananas being mixed with the sultanas.
Lactose is not used for a dry, Graves-type
wine.

Index of Recipes